I0204658

Child of the Brown Earth

by

Penny Kelly

Other books by Penny Kelly:

The Evolving Human

The Elves of Lily Hill Farm

Robes - A Book of Coming Changes

Getting Well Again, Naturally

Consciousness and Energy, Vol. 1

Consciousness and Energy, Vol. 2

Consciousness and Energy, Vol. 3

CHILD OF THE BROWN EARTH
by
Penny Kelly

Lily Hill Publishing
32260 - 88th Avenue
Lawton, MI 49065
info@pennykelly.com

ISBN: 978-0-9632934-8-0

Book and Cover Design by Penny Kelly

·Dedicated to
the
Great Mother of all,
our Earth·

Table of Contents

The Ancient Road

One night gazing at the sky
an ancient vision did appear,
a road so lonely, long, and dry,
stretched across ten thousand years.
On that road a figure moved,
walking slowly, head bowed low,
no one there to guide or soothe,
share a smile or wipe a brow.
Wanting so to comfort her
my heart reached out
through years of space,
"Would you like a friend to be with
in that dim forsaken place?"

Just a bit the footsteps faltered,
shivers shook the fragile form,
sending anxious waves of silence
filled with hope and doubt forlorn.
Wanting so to ease her sorrow
quick went forth the potent thought,
"Look around, look up, you'll see me...
I am with you...just believe."
Turning then, reluctantly
for one brief moment face upheld,
gazing at the apparition
in frozen shock I saw myself.

Confusion, fumbling everywhere
the vision faded into dark.
Dancing stars and moonless heavens
echoed through my aching heart
where now there runs an ancient road
through a place called time and space,
on that path a dogged soul
slowly moves without a sign
of self-reflection, recognition
or the hope of judgment fair,
there is only quiet movement
to a place she knows not where.

No Time for Gardens

In the early morn it is too wet,
later in the day it is too hot,
midsummer weeds are much too much,
there's money 'round the corner and we just
can't stop.

Schedules inhale every hour,
like sheep in the noose,
we run to the slaughter,
each day is a mirror of trivial pursuit
by men and women who love their suits.

No more do we come to March and plant
the food to sustain us when the system can't.
It's not our job to sweat or weed,
believe in Nature, or trust a seed.

No one cares 'cause no one knows
how deeply connected we are to soil.
Mother Earth has been replaced with
a madcap dependence on gas and oil.

Muddy Mess

Oh Earth,
my Earth
with your birds and boughs
I feel your touch,
feel you clutch
as I walk through
your wetness,
feel you squish
between my toes and
suck at my sole
crying,
"Look at the muddy mess
you people have made of me."

Lawn Care

Bits of leaf and twig
fall from my hair,
scratches sting on legs
that should have been
covered,
an itch that could be poison ivy
drives my right elbow mad.

The grass lies in hay-sized
heaps across the yard,
evidence of what
some call lawn care.

The decapitated clovers,
chopped bees, homeless
bunnies, routed chipmunks,
severed tree limbs, diced
mushrooms, and dying
grasses think otherwise.

At what point did
we begin
lying to ourselves
that so much destruction
was any form of care?

Penny Kelly

Hello Ivy

Our second meeting has been
disastrous as the first.
How dare you sneak across my skin,
burning, itching,
driving me mad
with discomfort
at the very moment when I must appear
sedate, sane, deeply conscious
before the viewing audience, and
instead I am
fighting an out-of-control itch,
an urge to scratch, totally distracted
by furious patches
of red hot cells.
Why my body? Why my life?
What is your purpose?
What's that you say?
I'm sure you are lying!
I do not blindly tread
where I do not belong.
I am sure your presence is more
nuisance than message...I think,
and your claims of
enlivening consciousness
only irritate.

Life and Death

In the early dew they were little and soft,
ten bright balls of yellow down,
blue eyes, huge and awkward feet
supervised by a gander guard
marching though my flowered yard.

We herded them out, Lindy and I,
barking and shooing
as they hissed and cried.
Down the hill and across the drive
until they were back through the
pasture gate, safe and sound
where they would not stay.

By high noon they were cold and still,
stiff and floating, matted down,
six of them already drowned.
Three were struggling at the edge,
one was sinking, close to death,
fighting the cold, reaching for breath.

Without the firmness of the earth
to offer them a gradual depth,
they ended trapped at the poolside lip,
too small to escape without a lift,
no well-oiled feathers to keep them dry,
just frantic parents who honked and cried.

Differences

What is the difference between:
Humans and crows?
Crows have strategy.
Humans and dogs?
Dogs have unconditional love.
Humans and snakes?
Snakes are flexible.
Humans and cows?
Cows don't eat us.
Humans and cats?
Cats can't be herded.
Humans and coyotes?
Coyotes sing to the moon and stars,
while people seldom sing to anything.
Humans and chickens?
Chickens don't pretend there is no pecking order.
Humans and alligators?
Not much, both bite when provoked.
Humans and most animals?
People talk to animals as if these furred and
feathered friends will understand
and they often do.
Animals talk to humans
but no one listens.

The End of Our Affair

Don't tell me you
are leaving already,
the cicadas have only
just begun to sing.
I love your sunny face,
your warm and smiling
breezes. I love your
flowery summer dress and
that wild green
ocean that moves in fluid waves
when the wind sings
and storms march
and you wrap your
sweaty arms around me the
moment I step out
the door. Don't leave
your leaves upon
my step like
scattered mail announcing
the end of our affair,
telling me that I should prepare
for your colder
older brother.

Too Late

Pink light fading, fields scorched
dripping eaves around the porch,
drops of moisture much too late
to wash away her hungry ache.

Swollen river, mildewed yams,
drying mud across his land,
waiting in a tent-filled camp,
spirit mouldy, chilled, and damp.

Frozen sidewalks, hoarse sighs,
pilfered lumber feeds her fire,
cardboard ceiling loaded with snow
flies toward heaven when the first wind
blows.

Forbidden substance, anxious snort,
he skims through meetings and board reports,
heavily armored with powder and power,
ignoring the fact it is all going sour.

Wild wind raging, broken glass,
family huddled against the blast,
trees in matchstick form are strewn
across the yard and living room.

Swirling mists, ambushed cars,
blood-stained bodies, door ajar,
tools, machinery left on order,
sit and rust at angry borders.

Silted streams, polluted seas,
big Cats treading through the trees,
strange bacteria once set free
change the course of history.

Rings of fire, melting trees,
haunted eyes of honeybees,
shriveled flowers, panting hawks,
panicked humans finally talk.

In the Cross-hairs

Man, hunter of the young,
the helpless
furred and feathered creatures,
stalker of his fellows
both friend and enemy,
watching with cunning clarity
each move his prey will make,
now fails to note
that nature has him
in her cross-hairs,
silently watching each
ignorant decision,
preparing to roll
her own plan forward,
setting his backward
thousands of years.

Pause

In the gray chill of Sunday dawn
a clock stares blankly from the wall,
one tiny light shines down the hall,
birds sleep, wrapped in snowy firs,
sunflower seeds wait silently in the feeder,
snow lies motionless where it fell,
trees reach nakedly toward a frozen heaven,
sun rises unseen toward the horizon,
nothing moves around or in her
except breath and the thought of death.

Don't Play Me False

Don't play me false,
I know your soft caress
upon my cheek
and the warm breath
that flows across my neck
is only a temporary mood.

Don't lie to me
in sighs that say
how much you long to stay
or with eyes that sparkle brightly
in the dark and yet in
daylight have gone away.

Why does your sun
shine down on me
with the promise of warmth
that's hollow?

You give me hope
but withdraw it all again
when in the weak light of dawn
I wake to find you gone,
my shoulders cold and chilled
for winter has returned,
it was only the January thaw.

Penny Kelly

Bergen-Belsen

Like a guard at Bergen-Belsen,
into the oven...slam the door...
start the fire and
never give thought to who
they were or where they came from,
did they have dreams or
unfinished business
before they fell to our
righteous demand for heat and light
because they could neither
run nor hide.
Even though they were living beings
it never occurs to us to ask
were their seeds all planted and
their saplings all raised,
how that unfortunate saw
came into their lives, or
where they fell to take
one last sad look at the sky.
How can we claim the
higher ground when we never bow
to these great beings and
seldom offer gratitude
for the gift of warmth we take?

A Warm Winter

Even a warm winter is
hard to recover from
when all your friends
have flown
south,
crumpled and
collapsed
at the first frost, or
faded
into gray skeletons
with the loss
of their green dresses.

Sudden Snap

The sudden snap,
the angry bite,
as if to say
you are not right
in your perception
or your heart
and they've a right
to throw a dart
that wounds and
stings especially when
your guard is down and
you did not
expect a frown.

Birds Do Not Sing

Birds do not sing
when volcanoes erupt,
animals abandon all routine
just before the earth quakes,
while humans march
noisily
arrogant,
into self-assured
destruction,
dumb as doorknobs
opening to dark chaos,
sauntering in
as if they owned
the darkness.

Shake, Rattle, and Roll

Look at the mess you made with
all that shake, rattle, and roll business!
Who is going to clean up those
bricks and boulders, and
what a waste of good trees!

Don't tell me that you tried
to wash away the mess
with those gigantic waves that
only made things worse
'cause now we have muck
upon rubble
upon remains
both human and animal

soon-to-be skeletons
tucked between stainless steel
dishwashers
perched rakishly next to
naked plumbing and a

once-blue, sateen-covered
king-sized mattress protected
by Scotchgard warranties
that float in yonder ocean or

perhaps just down the street
that no one dares to navigate
because the smell of death,
and wet burning vinyl is too much

for those whose communities
disappeared in spite of
prepper activity,
as the one thing for which
they failed to prepare
was Mother's local reality.

Unknown Ache

Each dawn I enter the newness
where faint pink mists
of anticipation
drift.

Each noon I rush toward calls and tasks
as if wondrous rewards
and savvy acclaim wait 'round
each bright and shining
corner.

At sunset I dawdle
as tinges of red-orange
color the sky but never
come low enough to
color my world
where horizons remain
flat and gray
as the curtain lowering on the day.

In the midnight shadows sadness settles,
veils of hurt fog fill the room.
Slowly I crawl into bed
where old aches wrap
around my soul
that went another day unfed.

Concocted Reality

You did this, didn't you...
wrapped these bones in flesh's finest,
slapped on eyes, a nose, and ears,
planted teeth,
attached some feet
and left me to wander
in fields of feeling,
crowded with others
more lost than me
who cannot hear
and will not see
the cause of their reality.
They travel confused,
drag me along,
destroy obvious truth
with homemade fictions,
leading us all
into temptations
that deliver us far from
core common sense
to arms
of concocted reality
that exists because we are powerful,
but lack any power to sustain existence.

Penny Kelly

No Answer or Excuse

Sit me down by October window
where wind and I can talk once more
before snow flies, burying hope
that summer's sun can last forever.

Walk me once more
through trees and fields
to cloudy doors
I thought were nailed shut,
shutting out the pain forever.

Sit me down on rolling
hilltop where fierce winds
hit full in my face
as newly red and golden leaves
turn and blow away,

leaving barren landscapes
without a place to hide
from the reverberating
Why-y-y-y?
that thunders lifetime
after lifetime when I

longed to travel and wouldn't,
wanted to write and didn't,

tried to love and couldn't,
worked to succeed
but was told I shouldn't

address the true spirit of self,
leaving that damnable,
low-moaning question
riding wild winds
flowing fast
through chilled houses,
forcing unsettled closure,
refusing to respond to truth and
having no answer or excuse.

I Am the Warp

I am the warp in the rug on the floor,
where everyone steps as they drift
through the door, noticing not
how I cushion their walk
or hide all the secrets I hear in their talk.

I am the hanger, the closet, the pole
waiting for life to give me a role,
to dress me in colors that sparkle
and drape over angular shoulders that
long to escape.

I am the sound of the tick in the clock,
the silence between that continues to mock,
the second hand sweeping around and
around, while time and illusion
keep keeping me bound.

I am the filly who sits at the track
cheering the horses that run like a pack,
dressed to the nines with her hair, hat,
and fringe, neglecting to cheer for
her own race or win.

A Living Space

Cups, bowls,
plates and pitchers
peer through cupboard glass,
chairs hold their seats,
tables stand at attention,
carpets lie,
sofas sigh,
curtains drift,
clocks tick,
spatulas gossip
to walls that laugh and
share their own tales
of what it takes to
be a container of human passion,
their hot frustration
watching our inaction
when we are so free
to move and do,
yet do so little while
they who hold space
remain
frozen,
able only
to peer, sit,
stand, lie,
gossip, tick,

drift or sigh
lest the ceiling fall
or chaos reign,
ruining our lives,
catching the blame for
failing to hold
a living space
for us
the half-alive.

A Haunting

A haunting, vague awareness crosses
o'er the threshold of my mind,
fills my soul with ancient aching,
seeks relief from humankind.

Soft and silent voices calling,
moaning through the sun-bright day,
sending chills that make me shudder,
crying that we've lost our way.

I move on, my hurried pace does
not admit the subtle trace
of knowing laundered histories,
squandered truth, and mysteries.

Where once there lived a vibrant culture
wise in spirit on an earth
of forest, sand, and sparkling sea,
sensitive and full of wisdom,
living, loving, laughing free,

now there toils a race of dullards,
gangsters, moguls holding debt, life
is chained in corporate prisons,
consciousness not ransomed yet.

Penny Kelly

No one questions past or future,
steel and glass are all they know
chasing the collapsing dollar,
glory, fame, and cookied heroes.

Slowly grinds the wheel of dust,
change is coming...
coming...

Come!
Be gone you
aching, lawless present,
rude illusion born of man,
mend the promise of the flower,
heal the place the oak tree stands,

let the quiet covenant
built within us loose the trap,
let the quiet fall around us,
let us feel the rising sap,
strength and power now connecting,
re-directing, infinite,
let us walk with deer and bear,
and with the stars be intimate,
living love and trailing care,
learning once again to share
all the Earth with furry others,
feathered, finned, sisters, brothers.

Raising the Half-Dead

Who will clear my calendar
from backlogged lists
where it lies caught
in meetings, calls and arguments
that while away my precious time?

What will wash me free of hurt
that fills the landscape
of my mind,
oozing doubt and loss and sighs
that muddy talk and cloud the eye?

When will we learn how to hear
beyond the world of
impaired hearts that
reach and smear and hit and grab
with touch that barely feels?

Who will take the body-mind
and zipper pieces into one
of consciousness and
rolling joy that
raises the half-dead to life?

The Lien

Slow, deep, targeted breath
flows through the body,
still,
at rest,
opening pathways,
bringing the light that
carries renewal
all through the night,
working around the
tensions and blocks,
loosening feelings,
untying knots
of anger, repression,
feelings and plots
subverting the body,
slowing the clock,
spinning the dreams
of useless success
that require a lien
on true happiness.

Kundalini

Sitting here with you inside me
I can feel your heat,
your warm tongues
moving like a wave along
the distance of my thigh,
my breast,
a momentary promontory,
curving, sweeping
chain of all-consuming fire
that takes me, bakes me,
shapes an unknown me
that stands so independently alive
each time my mind illuminates
a moment's truth or
sees a vision,
then the heat that has arisen
slowly burns away decision
and the time for full surrender
now surrounds
in white-hot grip,
alarming in intenseness,
it caresses silent tresses
that lie curling in the contours of
my shoulders, throat and neck,
while racing breath of searing pressure
pours through me an ancient pleasure

promising a conscious treasure
by the dawn's beginning breeze that
swirls away the ashes of a life
once lost in passion and
perspective that once fastened
all the tendrils of my mind
on the futile way I pine
for you
are life and I am fire,
lashed in your moment
I am kept
a shameless hussy begging
more
come heat the reaches
of my shores 'til I am
dampened to deep cores that
cry out
take me, make me
now
on surging waves of heat
I surf
through time and space
to reach the place where
up the distance of my thigh,
into my breast,
deep in my chest
a sweeping chain of
all-consuming fire
takes me, re-creates me.

Once Awake

Once awake, ears open,
you cannot help but hear yourself.

Once awake, eyes open,
you cannot help but see yourself.

Once awake, feeling expands,
you feel the cruel pain all around.

Then comes the mighty struggle with
the dogma and beliefs that you

can float above the fray, when
you can't because

the more you awaken,
the deeper you're in it.

Winds of Spring

Come a little closer,
wrap those wild wet winds
around my mind,
curl my naturally curly hair and
drench both cheeks
in dewy softness
long forgot in winter's grip.

Whip my skirts and plaster my shirt
against these breasts,
recovering shapes
lost for months
in bulky woolen layers,
reminding me of what a joy
it is to run,
hopping over rivulets
that flow down snow-plowed mountains
and across the asphalt plains
through grates that mark the straits
opening to the sewer sea.

Whistle brightly through the night,
shaking the shutters,
butting the doors,
trimming limbs
in the southeast quarter,

assuring Mother Nature's daughter
spring will be here soon,
tomorrow,
if not tomorrow then
the day that follows,
lifting drooping spirits
spinning them around,
filling hearts with warmth,
warming up the ground.

Firefly Light

Frogs sing
back and forth,
taking turns
filling the spheres
of yard and field
with rippling music,
inviting others
across the hills
to join the chorus
while I sit mute,
feeling acutely
ignorant,
inadequate,
not knowing how
to join their trilling
rhythmic songs.
When did we forget
how to trill, tweet,
moo, roar,
purr, bark,
howl, honk,
cluck, whinny,
growl, chirp,
and flash our firefly light?

There Was a Princess

There was a princess in my back yard.
She was *very* large and laid on her side
over by the wood pile
but was twice as long.
She wore a netted cap that sparkled
in the moonlight and
calmly gazed at me as if
we met every night.

"What are *you* doing here?" I spouted surprise.
"Just came to talk," she smiling replied.

Silent pondering from my hot tub seat
After a time, I prodded.
"Well, *speak*!"

"What do you want to know?" she asked
so politely.

More silent pondering on my part,
"I want the right questions...always,"
I sounded dubious, on shaky ground.
"No you don't!"
She laughed a bell-like sound.
"But I do, I do, I really do," came the weak
protest.

"How perceptive," she chuckled, "that's exactly the problem...your personal test!"

"Huh?" I grunted.

"You said *I do* and now it's in your way."
Her eyes twinkled,
but her mouth was very straight.

The silence deepened into
night wind and star song, with
chains of male conversation,
drifting upon them.

"No...no...no... (to everything I want to do)
"Where is the income ledger?
"Isn't that off-track for you? (raised eyebrow)
"How are you going to make any money at that?
"You'll see that's not really you if you'll just step back...
"That doesn't use the multiplier concept...
"What makes you think that's what you're good at?
"Now what *really* makes logical sense here?
"What are you trying to *do,* my dear?"

"Well?"
Once again, it was her turn to prod.

"I don't know what I'm doing any more...
I forgot... I knew once...before...
now my mind is caught in a stall.
Once I took direction from my heart,
now the bank makes the calls.
I've been struggling for ten long years...
tried it all...nothing but tears...
What am I doing here, anyway..."
This last was mostly a hopeless mutter.

Her mouth opened in a large, round O and
her eyes rolled a mercy-me glance
while a merry mourn rolled 'cross the land
and wrapping 'round me came her sound,
a command that cajoled and caught my soul
as the earth shook and the trees shivered,
the moon dimmed and inside I quivered.
"Tee-e-eaach-h!"
And in a silvery wrinkle, she vanished.

Prayer for the Little Light

A little light glows
in the middle of my table
like the little seed planted
in the minds of men at the
dawn of time.

A little flame dances
in the dark of my room
like the deep passion anchored
in the hearts of women
before Earth began.

A little Self sprouts into knowing
who we are,
causing music to sing,
setting waves of love ringing
to carry us toward
a newly restored
Earth and all her people.

Let the little light shine from
each and every one,
illuminating millions of
transformations.

Enter the Magic

How long has it been since you
stood in the seething darkness
watching fireflies,
falling into the magic of
innocence again.

The sun arrives at your door every morning
with warm greetings for a sunlit day
but you run rude
and heedless through it,
trailing currents of darkness and worry.

The world is starving for a smile and
what do you feed it?
Prickly perceptions,
seared meetings,
sour hours of competition.

Is this the way to repay
the loan of life made to you?
How long before the season is over
and your firefly light
goes out altogether.
Don't wait.
Enter the magic now.

Prayer of the Laundry Goddess

Let me roll through
the world
like a giant washing machine,
sloshing
away old life,
rinsing
the fabric of feelings,
spinning mortal appointments and
apathetic routines into a
whole new
being for reasons
of my own,
darning the week threads,
redressing
muddied thoughts and shapeless minds
'til they strut through
the world with a smile
full of faces
pressed and folded
in new directions.

The Sky Will Teach You Everything

The sky will teach you everything.
A jewel-blue sky full of
morning clarity turns to blue-gray
uncertainty in late afternoon,
the cycle of light
glaring, fading,
rain here and there,
thunder,
flashes of illumination,
autumn fog,
a shoulder of wintry frost,
snow jobs that are only fun
when you're young
and quickly become
working impediments
to shovel your way through.
Ice blue
followed by
powder-puff blue
changing to streaks and
clumps of watery blue gray that
sprinkle, dump,
even scour us with rain
then turn
and suck it all away again

in withering,
humiliating drought.
Look at that blue-black mystery
full of darting craft and
twinkling pinpoint planets.
Study that blue-black mystery
for the sky will teach you everything
you need to know about life.

Like a Nectarine Pit

Floods of knowing wash away nothing
by accident. They come only by
invitation from the hidden side
of the heart. Be ready
for rain and the hot roar
of the deluge in your
soul. Ride the white-water energies
into nothingness and
keep breathing
longer,
deeper,
wider
into that sound.
You cannot hold back those waves
of liquid light and expansion
that consume the little who
and what you were.
Let the flood snuff out your old self
then bring you back and
plant you
like a nectarine pit
in just the right place
for flowering and the grace
to be fruitful.

Crabby Rain

November skies hang low enough to
catch my curls
in gray, misty fingers
as a water-laden horizon
rolls toward us over the hills,
a frowning blue cloud
barely able to contain itself.

"No! Wait!" I cried.
"I'm not done
and we have an agreement.
I was out here by ten a.m.
and you said you
would let me finish.
I have only the screen house to cover,
the porch lights to change,
a cord of wood to move and stack."

At dark the work was done.
Within minutes the crabby rain
came shouting down,
complaining about how late it was.

Walk on the Wild Side

Let me walk
on the wild side
without excuse or apology,
dancing the white dance of
the wild heart that
refuses to stop
squirming,
insists on
running,
diving
into fearfully unknown
joys and passions.

Let unbridled winds spin
dervishes of tornado thought in
gales that sink
despair and
drown frowns
with total abandon.

It matters little that
fakirs in the temple
sell their illusions to fools.
These are merely
side-tracked paths
of the pinball machine of life and

I have learned to
shake the impudent table
and get away with it.

Let my heart pour
fast oceans of loving distraction
that flood the reality
like Noah's yarn,
making everything new again.

Woman-Eyes

Marcello suggested I talk to Mars
so gazing up from chilly step
in new moonlight I'm thinking,
"Where the hell is Mars...and could I see
more stars
out back, away from all these streetlights
and the glare of passing cars."

Fingers of day shrivel up into night,
in the dark the dim lights dance,
my life in review parades into sight
where memory's wand lends a softening
slant.

When suddenly shadow and gloom are alive,
along with the child of five inside
who was frightened of midget faery men,
pied-piper thieves and gray gremlins
with magical powers and musical spells
to capture the hearts of young children.

Shaking free of night-time's grip and
distancing my heart,
I return to my adult
with a different view of dark, as
a too-short time of desperate dreams

Penny Kelly

broken by days of grim routine
that slowly, methodically,
without cessation
lock lonely adults into meaningless creation.

Sadness trails along my spine,
I mourn for lost direction,
when vagrant thoughts from the
five-year-old child
provoke a chain reaction,
and reaching for that child
I find I'm groping in the dark,
a woman-child caught in stark
confusion as present and past
celebrate reunion
in a magic mushroom cloud of glee
when abruptly
the magic is stripped away
and we eye one another –
power and me.

Unbidden echoes pound my soul,
I hear breath sigh,
"Earth...you own me..."
as naive silence drifts away
replaced by thoughts of a bygone day
when I tried to renew the right to drive
without the license long expired.

I told them who and what I was.
"Prove it," they replied,
and I couldn't
because I didn't
have the paper that said I was me.
So I drove home illegally,
wondering
"Do I exist?"

Now it seems ridiculous
I ever tried to prove I Am
to the fools who reside
in illusion's land
where rigid is the law and
the faster you race,
the longer the shadows,
the deeper the daze,
the heavier the breathing
the sharper the pain
as the true self grinds down and
the magic drains.

But the spirit-child with the woman-eyes
sits still, awash in the spell of night
where second-sight
does away with the fright
of a pounding heart flooding lash to heel
with shivering, shimmering chant so real

that the rhythm words
I am...I am
resound with a message for all humans,
as the woman-child with the spirit-eyes
sits frozen on the step,
peering through time
at the children of the planet
flying on the run,
marching to the beat of an
unknown drummer's drum,
crouched in the murk cast by
dead o' night magicians,
frightened by the faery men,
unable to listen...

listen to their souls,
let fly the winged wishes
that open magic doors
away from dark magicians,
in to enchanted kingdoms
where the spirit-children run,
dancing in the warmth of
the razzle-dazzle sun.

I Am the Magdalene

How dare you Simon Peter
step upon my cloak of red
or cast away the sun and moon
that sparkle 'round my head.

How dare you Paul of Tarsus
masquerading through the land
insist that I keep silent
and that my head is man.

Shame on you O Roman Church,
the rock on which you lie
is but a millstone 'round my soul
that centuries has cried

as burning women died in sorrow,
martyrs sighed the last of breath,
papal spies and mercenaries
painted Europe with your death

while lowly men without esteem,
common men who claim God's seed
raise themselves above all others,
all for power, all for greed.

You Roman bishops quiet down
and bow in all subjection,
suffer a woman to teach you how
to recognize correction.

Correct yourself great Oxford book,
you know not whence you speak,
for Magdalene needs no reform,
your 'harlot' is a queen.

Shut your mouth, Tertullian,
you have no more to say,
a woman calls across the land
and claims her power today!

Breathing in the Night Wind

Wrapped in quilts,
warm,
not sleeping,
'cross the grasses night winds sigh,
calling, pulling,
"Come, my friend,
come and sit with me a while."

Toward the dark porch feet maneuver,
outstretched arms replacing sight.
Merging is the way of greeting winds
and dark and womb of night.

So we sit and breathe together,
I breathe out, she breathes in,
sucking herself back and forth,
wind and breath becoming one.
Slow...a new perception dawns
bright and shocking, always there,
we live each in one another,
she in me and I in her.

No wonder we've been such good friends,
knowing what the other needs,
listening to each other's stories,
sharing cold or warming breeze,

traveling round the globe we move,
messengers delivering seeds,
bringing news and rain and change,
breathing all her family.

Laughter giggles in my middle,
starlight twinkles in the tree,
night wind exhales in my nostrils
pushing, pulsing suddenly,
laboring and moaning low,
panting, sighing, still exerting,
exhales into my left nostril
giving birth to Earth in me.

Rocking backward with the weight
of the planet in my belly,
sore,
displacing heart and liver,
ragged lungs and breath now swelling,
gasping, asking my friend wind,
"Can she come out where she went in?"

Nodding like a trade wind hussy,
moving in a rhythmic dance,
"Breathe her into life..."
she coaches,
"Do it...do it..."
sings her chant.

Breath propelling all creation,
reaching deeply, up I thrust,
mountains scraping,
water splashing,
coughing, sneezing with the dust,
a world renewed to life now flashes.
Spent,
we rest in calm content.

Wind and I behold her beauty,
smitten by her blue-green shape
rocking slowly in the heavens,
swaddled in a cloud-like cape.
We croon a cosmic lullaby,
coaxing those first wobbly spins,
wooing birds and suns and rivers
'til she mothers us again,
calling with her many voices,
juice of life upon our chins,
wrapped in webs of many colors,
breathing in the night wind.

Spirit Stars

One luminous night when frost
had killed the last lone leaf on garden stalks
and stiff tomatoes slumbered cold and red
beneath old stakes,
a spirit star stood winking
where sweet onions months ago had grown
though nothing now remained but lumpy
dirt and thin, crisp skins.

The pea fence and the parsley
fluttered lightly in the night breeze as
she stood in upstairs window
staring hard into the dark.
A little star blinked back at her
from the garden far away,
twinkling on and off
in a highly intelligent way.

Throwing off a doubtful shroud,
she smiled and winked and spoke aloud.
The rosemary plant heard her say
excitedly and clear as day,
"The tools are nestled neatly
on the great hooks in the shed,
and neither hoe nor shovel
could reflect that errant light.

Must be that I am blessed
by something magic from the skies...
a spirit star come stealing from
the other side of night!"

She turned away in silent glee
at special stars, perhaps from Mars,
that came to newborn gardens
bringing omens of good luck;
took comfort in the quiet thought,
"Such spirit signs the gods have wrought
are badly needed in a world of logic
lost from common sense!"

Then went about all autumn
feeling smug and quite serene,
while the wind pushed rudely hard
at the silver can who played a star
until it rolled away on through
the silent, stubbled hollows.
Now legacies of spirit stars
live on as myths of favor,
tending blessed gardens growing
through all the springs that follow.

To Eat the Moon

An almost-full October moon peers down
through rain-chilled mist
where I stand gazing,
aching
with the hungers of the night.
Then slowly reaching up and up
I pluck the sky-ripe light and suck
the juice of brilliant moonbeams
mixed with
sweetened golden bites
of moon in melting mouthfuls
that burst across my tongue
and fill me up and up
'til moon and light and I are one.

My Former Me

Let me hear you, Mistress Wind.
Don't you know how
desperate I am
for natural familiars?
Let me feel you in my hair,
in my mind where
strange gusts
have blown away
the last loud structures of
old mainstays,
littering my inner lands with
snippets of code,
buttons and clicks
that carry me away to
page worlds that shift,
offering two-dimensional fun
that feeds to the point of
eternal hunger,
drags my soul forward, up and down
dropping me on unfamiliar ground,
scattering selves across a new time that
echo in a web-shaped mind
no longer appropriate for
earlier versions
of my former me.

Penny Kelly

Mother Nature, MBA

Carefully we write the vision,
state the mission,
plan the goals.

Businesslike we schedule seeds,
push the plants,
try to dance
in step with that great Mother
who
never worries
or even bothers
with payment dates,
overdue fees,
clocking in,
or salaries.

Yet when it's time to tally up,
the power of this partner's clear,
without a single MBA,
Mother Nature has no peer.

No one else puts heart and soul,
gives her all,
demands no role
except to be allowed to grow
your investment four hundred-fold.

Molecules of Emotion

Will they ever understand
there is no
feeling
without the hand
of chemistry,
and stuffing self
with factory foods
produces manufactured
perceptions and moods,
mass molecules of
predictable emotion
designed for behavior
shrewdly controlled
by those who crave power,
the fake puppeteers
who live behind curtains
and play on our fears.

House of Perception

Who remembers how it is to see
through time and space,
commune with owls and elephants,
sing to water, gather the mists,
or ask the trees,
to show the way,
then understand
when they talk back.

How many thank the studs that hold
the roof that keeps the rain out of beds,
off their computers, out of their hair
while feeding rivers and trees so fair?

Does anyone celebrate the date
those trees were cut,
milled, and shaped
into something they never
dreamed of being?

Who remembers the birth of those boards
into a life of commodity,
of service and work
never more to be seen
for who and what they were?

Who greets them, thanks them
as they arrive
at construction sites
where they are piled
to be measured, cut,
hammered,
forced
into labor
a century or more,
away from family,
friends, and fun,
unable to reproduce or
enjoy the stars and sun.

"It is only lumber,"
we say
because we are
civilized.

No more do we remember
hot nights
gathered in the moonlight
under spreading trees,
to dance, laugh, eat their fruit,
and lay among gigantic roots
holding us like tender hands while
we made love with
wild abandon.

We pull the shades now,
lock the doors,
have quiet sex for fear
someone will hear,
forgetting
everything is alive,
conscious,
communicating everywhere,
especially the trees
hiding in the walls,
holding our spaces,
remembering old places
longing for freedom
and a way of life long past,
taking small pleasures in
some semblance of the past,
dreaming of a future when
they are free and
we the people
might finally see
that all along
we were living and loving
in a fully aware
house of perception.

Frogs in Spring

I hear the sad voices,
long wails of despair,
tart snaps of anger,
hushed whispers
of hope,
the shaky
voice of authority, the
resentful jive of the young
mixed with short reports
of guns,
the silence of distrust,
and the shaming scorn
of disapproval coming
from everyone
everywhere.

Yes, the climate is being changed
in all of us.
We are under
threat from neighbor,
kin and
deep self within.

It matters not whether
money fails, food nourishes, or

nations implode, for
the landscape of the future
remains
shrouded in watery darkness.

So be like frogs in spring
and sing
in that damp darkness.
Whether you are peeper
or bullfrog,
your voice comforts the earth.

How to Dance

It never seems
as if we can,
it always seems
as if we can't,
but all will only
surely
be lost
if we forget
how to dance.

She Who Watches

Who pays tribute when a loving sky
spreads a golden quilt on high
of pin-tucked clouds to provide a shroud
that keeps us warm as the sun goes down
and the chill goes up?

Who applauds when a blackbird choir
serenades from the tree with
a passion so sweet that your
heart aches and your eyes leak?

Who thinks or cares when they
drive across fields
that beetles full of life and sass
are crushed as tons of rubber and glass
bear down on the victims
the way a dam
burst is never expected by the
life downstream?

Who thanks the sun for coming up,
asks the wind for favors or
enjoys a strawberry sup?
Who joins the conversation between
sand and sea or
falls in love with blackberries

enough to commit to
relationship with them
and their sprawling families of cane?

What will become of those who pretend
She never gave birth to us,
hasn't fed us,
doesn't watch over us till the end?

Perhaps
She Who Watches us
ignorant fools
knew we would return
after flaunting all the rules.

Psalm of Celebration

Joy sings me,
unrestrained
music dances me
voluptuously,
beautiful awareness
shouts from the life
overflowing from every corner.

The ant on my bathroom floor,
the moth in my closet,
welcome guests
for whom I roll out the red carpet,
bring out the best china,
hire the best dancers,
toast these companions of
living consciousness come to
grace my space.

Every leaf and blade of grass
is a masterpiece
worthy of framing.
Every bird deserves an
audience of thousands
for even a single note
and I am smote into
hypnotic bliss each time

the wind whistles and
whips the fires
of transformation and change.

I walk your hills and the
soft resistance of your contours,
weep in ecstasy
at the touch of that great light
shining from above, within,
and around all,
sigh in relief at the green and gold
moisture of shadows.

Oh let me walk here without
trampling a single flower, grain, or soul,
leaving only a trail of
small joys for others
to find and feel and feed upon.

Let my heart strew bits of love
for the millions of
Hansel and Gretel children
who have lost their way
and forgot how to recognize the
breadcrumbs that lead to the
bliss of the deep self.

Half Moon High

Half moon high
in a silver black sky,
cold crisp wind
floats across the night,
two furry shadows
race and run
in wild abandon,
full of some
enormous joy
that humans lost
in mad confusion,
work, and lust
for trinkets, toys, and
things that make
for pompous selves
that aggregate
in places thought to be
so fair
soul never will be
welcome there.

Full of Poses

When I was younger and deeply frenetic
the luxury of standing still
was out of reach,
beyond the means of my
emotional budget.

When I was younger and much too rigid
the pleasure of a sideways stretch
could bring on uproar.
Had I gone too far,
lost control,
or sacrificed those social nods?

When I was younger and oh so upright,
the flex and feel of
bending over
to moon the world
was quite improper,
a tasteless cosmic joke.

Now I am old and full of poses.
stretching, reaching, mooning, breaking
all the rules to open and flow with all
the rut-less, riotous power of
ancient living energies.

Penny Kelly

Calling All Fires

Here comes my friend
the great sun
made of
god-stuff
shining with all
the fire of life,
poking at the wind,
glancing off the waters,
throwing light everywhere
like a drunken sailor
on the solar sea,
warming the worlds,
calling us all
to life and warmth and
our own fire,
however small or large
that may be.

Splattering Gratitude

It started quietly from my bed,
a prayer of silent gratitude,
full of thank you's for
body, health,
food to eat,
even some ice cream,
a house with heat,
roof without a leak.

Moving deeper into the mood,
a distinctly energetic gratitude
for children, friends,
for clients, cash,
new internet service
coming in spring,
no metering or limits
and speeds that exceed
fifteen megabytes per hour.

The gratitude grew
with some real noise and sass,
calling to windows, walls, and glass,
boilers, chimney, floors, and doors,
bubbling with joy
they were in my life.

Suddenly the space was alive
with their voices,
as snaps, pops, and crackles,
even oilcan-like noises
added their song
of gratitude to mine,
creating a cacophony of
grateful replies.

Now carried away
by riotous joy,
I was
hanging out the chimney,
waving at the stars shouting,
"Hello Moon! Hello Mars!
I love you Big Dipper and Orion,
I love all you spaceships
and alien passersby!!"

Of course, they stopped, shocked,
swung round and stared
as if I were drunk
or emotionally impaired,
for they are not used to
those who communicate
let alone celebrate
by splattering gratitude
across the great skies.

Child of the Brown Earth

Once upon a time,
long ago
and not so far away
we danced upon it,
sang, and made love
to it each day.
Today we turn away
nose wrinkled with distaste,
suck it into screaming
vacuum cleaners
to be disposed of as if
it did not belong in our lives.

Will you wait until
they bury you in it
before you remember
the web of soil
from which you have
built yourself?
Child of the brown earth,
you have inserted yourself into
a borrowed collection
of earth-born minerals and
now strut about
as if no allegiance is due.

Penny Kelly

Thank you for reading these poems.
It is my wish that we can soon
come to recognize and
celebrate the life – seen and unseen –
that surrounds us all!

Penny Kelly

Penny Kelly, N.D. is a teacher of consciousness, writer, international consultant, speaker, publisher, and Naturopathic physician. She is the owner of Lily Hill Farm and Learning Center in southwest Michigan where she teaches and writes. She has been researching consciousness, cognition, perception, and intelligence for over 35 years. You can find more information on her website:

www.consciousnessonfire.com

www.ingramcontent.com/pod-product-compliance
Lightning Source LLC
Chambersburg PA
CBHW051700040426
42446CB00009B/1224
* 9 7 8 0 9 6 3 2 9 3 4 8 0 *